Staci's Little Book

You're More Than Average

Experiences that led me to a happier life

STACI INEZ

STACI'S LITTLE BOOK

YOU'RE MORE THAN AVERAGE

Published by Lee's Press and Publishing Company
www.LeesPress.net

This document is published by Lee's Press and Publishing Company located in the United States of America. It is protected by the United States Copyright Act, all applicable state laws and international copyright laws. The information in this document is accurate to the best of the ability of Staci Inez at the time of writing. The content of this document is subject to change without notice.

ISBN-13: 978-0999310342 *Paperback*
ISBN-10: 0999310348

Table of Contents

Dedication

To everyone I've encountered in life that helped shape my experiences, whether good or bad; I thank you.

What is happiness and how do I find it?

Merriam-Webster - definition of "happy" a : enjoying or characterized by well-being and contentment

There's obviously no formula for happiness, but it seems we are always searching for an answer. Happiness is everywhere - but the first place you should find it is inside of you. I can't tell you how to be happy, but I'll let you into my life so you see how I manage to remain happy. It may work for you, or you may think I have horrible ideas, but the point stands that no one can define your happiness for you. This is why it's important to spend time getting to know yourself. You have to spend time understanding what you like and don't like, what your strengths and weaknesses are, what makes you uncomfortable, and what makes you feel good about yourself. There are many ways to do this. For me, I love taking a walk through a garden or sitting by the lake. I also enjoy taking a journal and writing how I feel about life as a reflecting moment.

However you take time to get to know yourself, just make sure you do. Then, you'll begin to understand what happiness means to you. We're going to go on a more detailed journey in this book about what happiness is for me. Hopefully, you find something you can connect with to use in your own life and we'll share our happiness together by the end of this book. I'm really honored you're taking the time to read with me and I'm excited to share my experiences with you!

Stress is a choice

"The greatest weapon against stress is our ability to choose one thought over another." - **William James**

I'll never forget the day one of my fellowship colleagues asked me how I remained calm when I should have been panicking trying to meet our deadline. She went on to tell herself aloud "Be Staci. Be peaceful." She gestured her arms in a way that one would do if they were trying to calm themselves down. It was quite humorous at the time, but it also made me think about many other times people have asked me questions about how I remain so relaxed and stress-free. This doesn't mean that my life is perfect or that I don't get worked up about things; this simply means I don't allow these situations to cause a whirl of hell in my life. Often, people think I'm lying about not being stressed, but it really is an achievable goal **if** you change your thought process.

Take the following quote with you everywhere you go: "You have to change the way you think if you want to change your life." Though I wish this was my own quote, it's not, but this quote applies to literally any aspect of life.

Follow this example: You are at the mall, searching in circles for a parking space. You finally see one that's pretty close to the entrance, and you race over to grab it. You have your turn signal flashing to let other drivers know you are preparing to take the parking space, but one irate driver decides to take it from you anyway. Instead of losing your mind about the jerk who took your parking space that was so conveniently placed near the entrance, perhaps think about the fact that you've been wanting to get in more exercise or maybe even drop a few pounds. When you think about your situation this way, you can silently thank the jerk for taking your parking space, because now you're able to get your mini exercise for the day. Of course, you're not going to get a full workout or drop three pounds by walking from your car to the entrance, but you WILL gain a sense of peace knowing that you didn't lose your mind over an idiot and a parking space. Obviously, this example is relatively small, but I want to illustrate how simple it can be to change the way you think in a situation. I say this to myself all the time: "Staci, you cannot change what has already happened, so figure out a solution and move forward!" I promise this is the key to my stress-free life! Those 16 words help me keep my cool in situations that would otherwise call for immense stress.

Let's look at another, more elaborate, example: A couple months after moving into my first apartment, I got sick more than I ever had before. It seemed like I was sick at least three days in a row every week in the month of June. I was working at Duke University, which was such an awesome job, by the way!

Living in my first apartment also meant living with bills, so missing work was not the best thing in the world for me because that meant I was missing money. Missing money was obviously terrible because I was still spending money; spending money on visits to Urgent Care, spending money on various medications, (including medication that was prescribed to me months ago for something random that I did not need at all!), and spending money on food because I was usually too tired/sick to cook. I had insurance, but of course, that only reduced, not eliminated my prices. So, it's easy to see how my spending numbers added up quickly. I should mention that in May I came up with a pretty elaborate budget plan for June, July, and August detailing how much money I was going to spend on recreation, bills, food, gas, etc., and how much I was going to save. I was extremely proud of myself for this, because one of my goals in life is to keep my standards high, and my credit score higher.

With me being sick, missing work every week, and having bills to pay, I could have easily lost my mind. For anyone who has lived on their own, you know it can be frustrating to spend money when you're not earning money in return. However, I had to remember to treat this situation like every other situation. There was nothing I could do about being sick and missing work because it was already happening. The only thing I could do was take a detailed look at my finances, re-budget, and move forward. Of course, this meant I had to be a lot more conservative in my spending than I originally planned, which is usually not an easy task. Some days were a lot harder than others, and I did have moments when I felt like I wouldn't be able to keep up with my payments. What kept me calm throughout this time is the fact that I had a plan in place. **When terrible things happen in your life, the only thing you can do is move forward. Even if you could go back and change things, why would you want to? We learn and develop our character during our worst situations, so no matter how hard it may be, embrace it as a learning opportunity and push forward in life.** Having a plan soothes my mind because I'm now more certain than ever that I am capable of getting through the situation.

Here's my advice on creating a plan to remain stress-free in a stressful situation: Thoroughly examine your problem and write down the cause. By the way, I'm a firm believer in writing things down because it truly makes it easier to think through your situation (I'll be getting to this in just a moment). When you write down exactly what caused your problem, it's much easier to begin solving it. **One key to remember is, to be honest with yourself in identifying the source of your problems.** Once you have identified the source, write down the outcome you would like and make a detailed list of every step necessary to get there (I wrote out every part of my budget that needed to be restructured and I figured out exactly what steps to take to stay below my spending limit and reach my savings goals). After that, it's go time. Put your plan into action and stick by what you set out to do.

This plan is obviously detailed for bigger life problems, but it can work in keeping your cool during situations like the jerk taking your parking space as well.

<u>Writing:</u> As promised, I'm going to let you in on how writing plays a big part in keeping me stress-free. First, I recommend every living human on the planet get a journal. Don't pick out any old journal, though. Really take time to browse for something that fits you; whether it be size, texture, design, etc. Find a journal in which you want to freely express yourself. One reason I enjoyed writing in my journal was that I loved the way it looked, and I loved how durable it was (believe me, you don't want a cheap journal). Writing is one of my many outlets of expression and I never overthink my sessions with my journal. I always let my mind and hands work freely and I don't stop writing until I have to force a thought. Once you get to the point where you need to force your thoughts, read over what you've already written, and see if anything else comes to mind that you should express. I always try to let my mind take over the writing session. I started by writing in my journal every night before bed. I wrote everything that occurred during the day and how I felt about it. The reason I write how I feel is that it gives me the chance to get to know myself a little more each day. This

gave me time to take a raw look at myself, understand how I think and process life's happenings, and most importantly, make sure my overall well-being was in check. My last point is most important because when I write, I have no filter, so I literally put down every single thought, feeling, or emotion that comes to mind. I am so busy/focused during the day that if something irritates me or makes me feel a certain way, I don't have time to fully acknowledge it or even dwell on it. But when I write in my journal at night, I have nothing else to do but write, so I have a chance to really examine how the situation made me feel, how I responded or didn't respond, and what, if anything, I can do about it. Here's what I would recommend: after you've done all the writing you can, go back over what you've written and have a conversation with yourself about it. It may seem strange, but sometimes what you need is to have a pep talk with yourself about what's going on in life and what you need to do to get where you want to be. Just try it! It's worth it. Remember, stress *is* a choice. **You may have stressors in your life, but you don't have to let them stress you out.**

Chapter Checkpoint

"The greatest weapon against stress is our ability to choose one thought over another." - **William James**

What are three things stressing me out right now?

_____

_____

_____

_____

_____

I may have stressors in my life, but I don't have to allow them to stress me out. What are three things I can do to change the way I look at the stress in my life?

_____

_____

_____

_____

_____

_____

_____

_____

_____

_____

_____

_____

_____

_____

_____

_____

_____

_____

_____

_____

_____

_____

_____

_____

_____

Get it together

*"Being organized isn't about getting rid of everything you own or trying to become a different person; it's about living the way you want to live, **but better.**"* –**Andrew Mellen**

Staying organized plays a major part in helping me maintain a stress-free and ultimately happy life. I can't tell anyone how to live their life, but I can tell you how I live mine and what works best for me. There are so many aspects of our lives that we have to keep up with, so I try to keep everything close together.

Bills, Bills, Bills (like the old Destiny's Child song) ... and other important things!

I keep all of my bills in an accordion binder and label each tab accordingly. Although I pay my bills online, I still receive a paper copy in the mail; whenever I need proof of residency or there is some type of billing error with a company, I have my own copy on file. Plus, I just like having the hard copy of important documents to avoid relying solely on technology to save our lives. Believe me, I am more than happy with the advancements in technology, but we all know if it can be built, it can be destroyed, and you don't want to be on the short end of that stick. Moving along, I moved into my first apartment a few days before I graduated college, and I made it my number one priority to maintain an awesome credit score, as I said before. For me to maintain an awesome credit score, I have to be organized. Not only do I keep a hard copy of my bills, **I also have a budget notebook to help me keep track of when I paid my bills and how much they were.** I often pay my bills early in the month, so when the actual due date rolls around, I freak out for half a second wondering if I paid the bill. Thanks to my budget notebook, I can see the day I paid the bill, and back to normal, I go. I also keep a general track of all my expenses in my budget notebook, along with my savings and other financial goals I have. This helps me see where most of my money is going and it helps me plan a budget for the next month. Of course, you can look at your bank statements, but for me, this is easier and I feel more accountable when I write things down. Budget notebooks aren't that expensive and you can find them in a variety of stores, so perhaps you can give it a try? You'll have to practice a little bit of discipline if you're someone who is very forgetful. If you forget to write down your bills/expenses, obviously it doesn't do you any good, but if you use it properly, the best that could happen is you take back control of your finances and eliminate some of that money stress. If you don't like physically writing things down, try creating your budget through the EveryDollar website/app. No one likes to pay bills, but bills won't disappear, so you might as well make the process as smooth as possible.

I have notebooks and folders for everything because I still enjoy physically writing things down, as you all know by now. The best way for me to remember a to-do list is to put it on paper; you may be the total opposite, and that is okay. If you're someone who likes to have everything on their phone, I'd recommend using the app Wunderlist. It's a to-do list app where you can create multiple categories and stay organized; you can use it on your phone or your computer and it's quite simple.

I also have an accordion folder for important things like insurance policies, documents related to my car purchase, medical papers, bank information, etc. This, again, is because I like to have at least one hard copy of my documents. I'm not saying you must have hard copies of everything; I'm just what some people would consider old-fashioned because I don't like relying too heavily on technology.

Being organized is so much more than a notebook or folder, though; it's a lifestyle, and it starts in your head. Having a sense of organization can tremendously help reduce stress. **When you're stressed about life and you can't seem to get organized, it makes everything else in life seem a lot harder, because now you're stressed about being stressed.** We've all experienced that feeling at least once in life, right? *raises hand*.

There are plenty of small things you can do each day to regain a sense of control in your life, and for me, writing is always my go-to. When I need to regain a sense of organization, before the day begins, I think about every task I'd like to complete before I go to bed, and I write it down. Then, I write down what steps I need to take to check that item off the list. Sometimes it helps if I make a weekly to-do list and then break it up by days. Let me show you:

This is an example of my weekly to-do list

May 21-May 27

-Go to post office

-Finish DIY project

-Schedule meeting with Vanessa

-Email contacts from LA event

-Go grocery shopping

-Pay bills

-Update website

Then, I'll assign different tasks to different days...

Monday, May 22

-Email contacts from LA event

-Go grocery shopping

Tuesday, May 23

-Go to post office

-Pay bills

-Update website

Wednesday, May 24

-Schedule meeting with Vanessa

-Finish DIY project

This is simply an example, and your to-do list may be longer, shorter, or totally different. Doing things this way helps me see the bigger picture first, and then narrow it down day-by-day. This is helpful for me because I can focus more specifically on one or two things at a time, versus trying to accomplish 30 things at once... meaning I'm much more likely to get things done.

Making your bed

On a very simple level, try making your bed every single morning. I've read many articles that suggest making your bed every day can help in your productivity. With or without the articles, I can say it certainly does help me feel a lot less cluttered and it gives me a fresh sense of energy for the day. It may seem like a small task, but making my bed improves the overall appearance of my room, which helps me think a little more clearly. I look at it like this: when the bed isn't made and there are sheets/covers everywhere, it's a representation of my mind. My mind is as cluttered and messy as the bed I haven't made. But when I *do* make the bed, my mind is as clean and neat as the comforter laid out evenly across the mattress. Now, I've set the foundation, and I am motivated to tackle whatever the day may bring. I know it seems small, but try doing it every day for a week, and see if it helps give you a clearer vision each day.

Routine

Another thing that can help with feeling more organized is getting into a routine. Whether it's your morning routine or a routine you use when you come home from work, having one might make you feel more productive. It could be anything from taking time to read a book before you leave for work to create a positive attitude, or running for 10 minutes around your neighborhood when you get home from work. It doesn't matter what you do and it doesn't have to be anything extensive, but having something you can do each day consistently (like making your bed every day) can help settle your mind a little and make you feel more balanced.

This is not an all-inclusive guide to a life of organization, either. These are just some ideas that have helped me stay organized throughout the chaos in life, but I definitely suggest looking into things that can help *you* feel more productive as well. When I need some organization inspiration, I browse through Pinterest because I always find cool life hacks about being more organized!

But if you don't take anything else away from this part of the book, at least remember this quote by organizational expert Andrew Mellen: "Being organized isn't about getting rid of everything you own or trying to become a different person; it's about living the way you want to live, **but better.**"

Chapter Checkpoint

*"Being organized isn't about getting rid of everything you own or trying to become a different person; it's about living the way you want to live, **but better.**"* –**Andrew Mellen**

What daily actions can I repeat to get into a routine and make my life a little less cluttered?

1. _____
   _____

2. _____
   _____

3. _____
   _____

4. _____
   _____

5. _____
   _____

6. _____
   _____

7. _____
   _____

8. _____

_____

9. _____

_____

10. _____

_____

Become a better you

*"Do not let the memories of your past limit the potential of your future. There are no limits to what you can achieve on your journey through life, except in your mind." –***Roy T. Bennett**

We spend so much of our lives working, so it only makes sense that hating your job could lead to hating your life. That can eventually affect your overall happiness, and that can easily create a downward spiral for your inner peace. Job searching can be one of the most exciting and stressful times in our lives. It's a time where you get high hopes and then get disappointed all in the same day because you found a good opportunity, but you never got a callback. OR maybe you've found your career and you've been with your company for a while, BUT you feel like all you do is go to work, come home, eat, sleep and repeat. I'm going to talk to you as well because there is more to life than your job and it's your responsibility to take advantage of all life has to offer. So let's talk.

The first key to job searching: Persistence! Before you even begin the job search, you have to tell yourself no matter what happens, you are going to remain strong throughout the entire process until you reach your goal. Of course, we'd rather be doing something more fun than filling out applications all day, but it's important to remember that nothing lasts forever. So your job search will soon come to an end because you're going to remain persistent, right? Great. It doesn't matter if you're fresh out of college, you've been working for years and need a new job, or you have a job but are looking for a second job. Maybe this is your first time looking for a job; no matter the situation, you have to remember everyone else is also looking for a job, so it's your responsibility to set yourself apart from the rest of the crowd. I once applied for a reporter position at a TV station. I emailed the news director of that station and when they responded back to me, I immediately told them I will come down to their studio and meet with them in person. They were very surprised that I was willing to come so soon, but for me, I wanted to make the best possible impression. So, the next morning, I hopped in the car and drove four hours so they could see me in person and see how serious I was about the job. I ended up getting the offer, but I had a couple offers that were a little better, so I turned it down. Needless to say, being persistent in your goals certainly pays off. Now I'm not saying you have to drive four hours or further to get a job. What I *am* saying is you need to show people you are serious when you're applying. No one has time or money to waste on you if you're not going to go hard at all times. You need persistence throughout this entire process. You need to put the persistent mentality in your brain before you start the job search. You'll need it during the journey as well to keep pushing forward, and you'll need it after you've done all you can to make sure people don't forget who you are.

"Chance favors only the prepared mind," said Louis Pasteur. When you're searching for employment, being prepared is critical. I've been told my entire life "if you stay ready, you don't have to get ready," and that is something I firmly believe in. You must be prepared at all times during your job search because you never know when opportunity will strike, and we know opportunity doesn't like to repeat itself. The first thing anyone wants to see when you're talking about getting a job is a resume. You have to make sure your resume is as updated as possible at all times. You don't want to be caught empty-handed when someone asks for it, but of course, in modern-day, we don't walk around carrying our resume. Of course, there are certain events or functions where you should certainly have your resume on hand, but on a regular day, it should be available online. Because of that, I would suggest building a website for yourself. You don't have to be a computer wiz to build a website, either, because there are plenty of sites that have simple, free templates for you to use. This way you can have everything you need in one place. You want to make sure you have your resume listed in plain sight and you want to make sure you offer an option for people to download your resume, in case they want to print it out. I also think it helps to have a professional photo of you as well. If you are trying to work in a field where you'll need to provide examples of your work, having a website is the place to put them. You can create a tab titled "Sample Work" to let people know where they can see what you've done. Also, it is crucial to have contact information on your site. If someone comes across it, they need to know how they can reach you if they're interested. After such a long job search journey, you'd hate for someone to pass up on giving you an offer because they couldn't get in contact with you, right? Have your phone number and email address available in plain view, and make sure it's accurate. You can add a lot of other information to your website, but you certainly need to make sure you cover the basics. You don't want your site to be too crowded with information because people won't even take the time to look through it. Make sure your fonts are clear and make sure your information has enough space to be read easily. And just like the resume, your site needs to be updated at all times, because you never know who's going to give it a look. Like I said before, there are plenty of templates for a free website, so perhaps you find one that's rather simple, yet professional, and add your personal touch. One important note in the preparation process: **make sure every single word is spelled correctly!** No one will excuse spelling errors on your resume or website because you have plenty of opportunities to look over it, and it shows that you are careless. So, let's remember the quote of the day: *"Chance favors only the prepared mind."* -**Louis Pasteur**

Now that we understand how important it is to be prepared at all times, especially while you're on the job hunt, let's talk about the process itself. Let's say you've just finished up with college and you're ready to put that degree to good use. You had a pretty decent GPA and got good training, but for some reason, it seems like no one in your career field is hiring. But how is this possible? You saw Melissa get a job in the same field you studied, so there must be openings; how did she find them, though? If this is close to the way you've been thinking, it's okay! There is no formula when you graduate that can calculate how to land a full-time job using your degree. Here's one thing I *do* know that makes a difference in your post-graduate success: networking! I will say, the connections I made when I was in school played a huge part in helping me start off on the right track with my career. So, if you're reading this and you're still in school, work with your professors and counselors, now, to establish good relationships that can lead to a career. But if you're not, networking is still very important regardless of your level of education. You have to put yourself out to people to let them know what opportunities you're looking for, and never be afraid to ask for help along the way.

It can easily seem like the world has nothing left to offer after you spent years and thousands of dollars on an education that was supposed to help make sure you got a job. That's when reality sets in that most people don't get that full-time, salary job in their field right away, and that is okay, too!

We all get that feeling of wanting to give up at some point or another, but often times we give up when we're so close to reaching our goal. If this is your situation, it's okay! **It's not about the situation you go through, it's how the situation goes through you.** I say that because no matter what happens in your life, the way you view the situation determines how it affects you. Your perspective can make what someone would deem to be a horrible situation, something beautiful. It's all about how you let the situation go through you. Remember that.

Networking: It's always a lot easier said than done when it comes to talking with people about job searching, but as hard as it may be, I'm here to tell you **if you stay hungry for success, you will eventually eat.** So let's talk about the networking I mentioned earlier. When you're looking for jobs, don't be afraid to talk with people you trust. Let them know what type of work you're looking for and ask them if they can put you in contact with anyone that can help. You never know who other people know in life, and that's why you need to put yourself out there. If you're attending an event or dinner, whether it's formal or casual, socialize with people in the room. Find out what they do for a living and see if you can make some connections to your goals. I understand you may not be an extrovert, but if you're looking for a job opportunity, you're going to have to break out of the shell a little and talk to people you don't know. **When you're talking to people about job searching, make sure you can clearly explain what you are currently doing and where you'd like to be. People respond better when you sound like**

you know what you want. Be able to talk about two or three things you've done that show you are capable of handling whatever type of work you're looking for. While I was working at one job, I decided it was time for me to move on because I didn't want to remain in a negative environment, while also becoming stagnant in my career (I have a lesson about this also, so stay tuned!). I started looking around for other jobs and I began talking with a few people to get my name buzzing. I have a degree in mass communication, so I told people I'm looking for a job in that industry. I started mentioning how I'd previously worked in a communications office, and I talked about the work I did for a university PR office as well. Doing this gives you more credibility, and people are more likely to help you when they hear you talk about relevant experience.

This doesn't mean you have to list off 7-10 years of experience, but mention a few things to demonstrate you know what you're doing. Every single job I've had was the result of talking to people and making connections.

Networking is made easier when you have a way for people to contact you, as I mentioned for your website. I would also suggest getting some business cards. It doesn't matter what your current situation is now, they are inexpensive and can help take your level of professionalism from nothing to something. After you finish telling people how great you are, you need to be able to hand them a form of contact so they can follow up with you. The last thing you want to do is ask someone if they have a pen and paper to write down your phone number and email address. Have those business cards handy and make good use of them. Give them to anyone who may be able to point you in the right direction, and make sure you get their contact information as well. You don't want to sit around waiting for someone to call you, so getting their business card will speed up the process a little, and again, it will show them you're serious when you reach out to them.

And after all of your hard work, you want to make sure you follow up with everyone you come in contact with. When you go to an interview, send a nice follow-up/thank you email to let the person know you appreciate their time and you hope to have the opportunity for employment with the company. Also, follow up with people you meet when you get their contact information; don't simply toss someone's business card after you meet them. Email or call them and set up a time for you all to talk more in-depth about their career and what you want to do in the near future. This is how you maintain the connections that may help you along the way.

"The quality of life is more important than life itself." - **Alexis Carrel**

Let's move to the other subject I mentioned at the beginning of this chapter. If you've been in the same job for years, but you feel complacent in life from being so repetitive, this part is for you. One thing to remember is that **you never have to settle for anything in life, no matter how old you are.** Just because all you do is go to work, come home, eat, sleep and repeat, doesn't mean you have to continue being that way. You have to take a look at yourself and find things that interest you to separate yourself from your work life. Think about things you used to love doing before you got settled into your current situation. Think about what hobbies used to excite you that you currently don't do anymore; anything from DIY projects around the house to blogging, or maybe you used to go for walks in the garden every Saturday. Really take some time to think about things that used to make you happy. You are never too old to get back into those things, and it's important to remember that your happiness is critical to your overall health and well-being. I always say my main goal in life is to have inner peace and happiness because I know everything else will fall into place if I have those two things aligned. A lot of us spend most of our lives working, but if you don't like your job, it's possible you may start to dislike your life, so **it's important to keep your work life separate from your personal life in some way.** You have to find an outlet for expression that can keep you motivated to be happy and stay happy. I use photography, dancing, and sports to take me away from any negativity at work. I've always loved to dance, so being able to do even a little bit of dancing makes me feel like there are no worries in the world. The same goes for sports. I play volleyball and soccer a few times a week to also free my mind. This way I don't feel like work is overpowering my entire life. I'm not saying you have to do any of these specific things, but you *do* need to find something that can get your mind off of work and restore a sense of peace and happiness to your life. This may also include looking for a new job. Maybe the reason you're unhappy in life is because of the job you currently have. Maybe your job doesn't allow you to step away from it, and you feel like you need a break. If that's the case, all the principles we went over earlier in the chapter still apply, because you're back on the job hunt like everyone else. **Life is too short to be doing anything other than exactly what you want to be doing.** You have to remember this whether you're in your 20s or your 60s. You have a purpose in life, you just need to find it. There's no need in spending time doing things that don't make you happy, jobs included. Of course, you need to be smart about your decisions. If you're going to begin looking for a new job, you don't need to let your current employer know, and you need to make sure you have enough money saved up in case you need to relocate. But make sure whatever decision you make is the best decision for your life. Get your energy back and begin taking control over your life.

So, whether you're on the job search, or you want to change career paths, remember a few principles:

-Persistence

-Preparation

-Networking

-Follow up

Don't be afraid to get out and try new things to enhance the quality of your life, either. **It's so easy to get caught up in working for a living that we sometimes forget to live for a living. You're already alive, so why not give yourself the best life possible**. There's more to life than your job, so I encourage you to get out there and find it. Good luck and keep your head up. You got this!

Chapter Checkpoint

"Do not let the memories of your past limit the potential of your future. There are no limits to what you can achieve on your journey through life, except in your mind." **–Roy T. Bennett**

Am I truly happy with where I am in life?

_____

_____

Where do I really want to be in life? If someone could hand me the opportunity I've been searching for, what would it be? And then let's think about what steps I can take to get to that opportunity.

_____
_____
_____
_____
_____
_____
_____
_____
_____
_____
_____
_____
_____
_____
_____
_____
_____
_____
_____

What new job opportunities can I take advantage of right now? Write down a list of potential jobs. Then put a check mark after you've applied and followed up with the company.

Job Opportunities	Applied?	Follow-up?

The Courage to Move

"Courage doesn't mean you're not afraid. Courage means you don't let fear stop you." –**Bethany Hamilton**

As we talked about earlier, I was working at Duke and a TV station the summer after I graduated college because I wanted to be a TV news reporter. Quick fact about me: I always I wanted to live at the beach. I grew up three and a half hours from the beach, so I knew the moment I had the chance, I would take it. I also knew I didn't want to live in North Carolina anymore because I had grown up there my entire life. Don't get me wrong, I love North Carolina, forever and always, but I knew I wanted to experience living on my own in a different state.

When it came time to start sending out my reporter demo reel in hopes of finding a job, I applied to five beach markets. I didn't want to go too far away for my first job, so I kept my options as close as possible, but just far enough.

I was working tirelessly at the TV station to shadow reporters and get field experience, so I could be as prepared as possible for my first job. December rolled around and I started sending out my demo. Because this chapter isn't dedicated to the process and persistence of my job search (see the chapter on becoming a better you), I'm going to fast forward to the relevant part. In January, I accepted a position to be the morning reporter at a TV station in one of the beach markets. FINALLY! I was excited to be checking off an item on my bucket list: to live at the beach. I was extremely excited, but from January 11th, I had two weeks to move down and get settled, because I had to start work by the end of the month.

I was excited at the idea of moving to a different state like I wanted, but I was sad to be leaving everything I'd known for the past 22 years. I moved about three and a half hours away from home and I couldn't have been more excited. It wasn't until a month or two into the job that I realized how much being away from home affected me in my daily life.

Now, three and a half hours is certainly not the same as me moving across the country, but the fact that you're able to move to a place where you don't know anyone is a big deal and it's' something for which you should be proud. However, I wouldn't dare lie and say it's easy -- because it isn't. When you move away and start a new job, it can be overwhelming. You're getting adjusted to a new city, you're learning your new job, it seems like life is coming at you in 10 different ways, and you're just trying not to get knocked out. The truth is that it's extremely tough when your job is demanding and you have no one there to physically support you. Many times you will want to give up and you will probably question why you even made the decision to move. You will feel like you were much better off in your previous environment of comfort. **But what is life if you only live it inside your comfort zone?** A musician once said, "The sooner you step away from your comfort zone, the sooner you'll realize it wasn't all that comfortable." This holds true in more ways than I can imagine. There is so much more to life than what you've known for the past however many years you've been alive, so never limit yourself in where you can go and what you can do. There were many times when I first moved that I felt like I wanted to be back in a more comfortable environment, with more friends and family around, but I knew that wasn't an option. So, I had to put my big girl pants on and tough it out. I have to give so much credit to my dear friend, Paula. She was one of the first people I met when I moved and she welcomed me so well. I talked with one of my coworkers about a cardio fitness class, and my coworker told me to come. When I went to the fitness class, I found a group of people playing volleyball (Paula was a part of that group) at the same gym. I asked around and found out when they typically play. The following week, I was playing volleyball and I started going three times a week. That's where I met Paula! I hadn't even been in the city a month, but she asked me to go Salsa dancing with her one Saturday night and I was totally down for it. When you move to a place where you don't know anyone, you can't be afraid to get out and do things you don't normally do. Of course, you need to be safe at all times, but you have to get out and meet people to make your new home feel more like home. That's exactly what happened with Paula and she literally became my best friend in the city.

I could've easily said no to the cardio fitness class, playing volleyball, and going Salsa dancing, but because I didn't, I began experiencing life in my new beach town and I started to feel more at home. This is extremely important when you move somewhere and don't know anyone because it is very easy to feel lonely. You'd be surprised what you'll get into if you step outside your comfort zone and just live a little. Moving away can be scary for many people, but it really enhances your quality of life. When you move to a new place, look for different Facebook groups that share similar interests as you. I found a group for people who play volleyball, and people who play pick-up games of soccer because those are some of the things I like to do. You can ask around and find just about anything, though.

In my case, I moved because my job took me, but if you're one of many people who just wants to start fresh or drop everything and move, I think that's great. However, if that's what you want, you need a solid plan in place. I totally understand needing a fresh start, but you will put yourself in a deep hole if you aren't prepared. If you want to move away, you should have enough money to avoid going into too much debt. It's also a good idea to make sure you have some type of employment lined up in the city you want to move. If you don't, then you definitely want to have enough money saved up to allow you to survive until you find employment. I've seen people I know decide they "needed something new," so they packed up everything one day, moved to another place, and wound up struggling because they had no real plan in place. They didn't know where they were going to work, they didn't have a solid place to stay, and they ended up living a worse life than they had before they moved.

One thing is for sure; no matter what your situation, if you have the courage to move away from your comfort zone and live somewhere else, you'll learn so much about yourself. You'll learn a lot more about who you are and you will begin to appreciate things about yourself you probably didn't pay much attention to before. For me, I was able to realize my own strength. When you're dealing with a demanding job, a negative work environment, and not having physical support in a new place, it can become really tough. But I was able to overcome those things without giving up or letting it break me down. If you decide to take a step and move to an unfamiliar place, you will certainly need to build a support group of some sort while you're there. It doesn't have to be 10 people, but even having one person you can lean on will make things easier.

Paula became a really good friend of mine, and my coworker, Sina, was also supportive because we shared the same challenges being in a new place. I ended up meeting the love of my life, Justin, as well, so between those three people,

I'd developed a core support system to help ease the challenge of being away from home. There were many days when I was overwhelmed with work and I needed an outlet to step away from it. During those times, I would go play volleyball or go see Paula, who is not only my friend but my pretend-therapist too. I would look forward to relieving any stress from my job on the volleyball court, and it was fulfilling having something like that to look forward to. My boyfriend and I worked for the same people, in the same career at one time, so it was very easy for us to understand each other and provide the support we both needed, despite living an hour and a half apart. Of course, you don't want to forget your friends and family back home that are always going to be there for you, but sometimes you need that physical contact from people nearby to keep you motivated and uplifted. Don't get me wrong, this isn't to say if you move away it will be horrible and depressing. It's a totally rewarding experience, and if you have a plan before you move, I think it would really benefit your life. What I *am* saying is if you move away from all the people you've known and the life you're used to, sometimes things can get challenging, and when that happens, it's important to have the right people around you to make things better. Not to mention, this is also the time when you'll have to build some pretty thick skin and learn to be tough for yourself. **When no one else can be there for you, you have to be there for yourself.**

Never be afraid to step out and chase your dream, even if that means moving to the other side of the country for a better opportunity. Just remember who you are and be open to all life has to offer.

Chapter Checkpoint

"Courage doesn't mean you're not afraid. Courage means you don't let fear stop you." –**Bethany Hamilton**

When is the last time I did something I wasn't totally comfortable with?

_____

_____

_____

_____

_____

_____

_____

_____

Stepping out of my comfort zone can provide a sense of accomplishment. What am I going to do in the next three months to take a chance on something I once feared?

_____

_____

_____

_____

_____

_____

_____

_____

_____

_____

SCOTUS - - - -> SCOSM:
The Supreme Court of Social Media

People have become so consumed with their virtual lives that sometimes they can't separate the internet from reality. Some people have become so comfortable hiding behind the screen of their phone, tablet, or computer, that they became uncomfortable in front of actual people. I believe anything that is good can also be bad in one way or another. So, why is this section referred to as The Supreme Court of Social Media? Well, because it seems that some people believe social media has the same value as the Supreme Court of the United States - the highest court in the land. I've never seen so many judgmental and, increasingly envious people until I began using social media. So, let's talk about some ways to step back from it all and live in the moment.

Don't compare your *real* life to someone's *virtual* life.

If you use the internet to prove that your life is just as "perfect" as someone else's, social media isn't for you. Sadly, many people do this without realizing. It's easy to portray a perfect life on the internet, but we know no one actually has one. It's okay to admit you are truly imperfect. **We all come with beautiful flaws that make us unique, so embrace them.** We've all seen people on social media who have, seemingly, flawless lives - and there is nothing wrong with that. The problem comes when you begin comparing your real life to someone's virtual life and try to portray an image that does not exist. I've seen people treat social media like the final word, and everything they do has to be validated by likes or retweets. I can admit, I've come across people on Instagram and I say "how in the world do they have their entire lives together?" I think it's completely natural to be slightly jealous of someone with a seemingly perfect life - especially when you're still trying to sort out yours. But here's the key: you truly have to accept that you will never be able to live someone else's life and there is nothing wrong with your life. **Let what you see be the inspiration for you to create a better life for yourself.** Seeing people do well for themselves motivates me to work even harder for what I want in life. I'm not comparing my life to theirs, but I'm acknowledging that I can be better than I am right now in some way. We have come to a place where people feel they cannot properly function without being active on social media. Celebrities can't take a break from social media without fans thinking they've died. *You* probably couldn't take a month away from social media without people wondering if you're on some deserted island with no technology. Now, this is not to say I hate social media at all. This is just me illustrating how serious this stuff is to a lot of people. Some have allowed their followers to become supreme court justices, voting on every decision you make. This type of thinking is harmful to our peace of mind for two reasons: It forms the impression that we have to live to please everyone else and not our ourselves, and it shows that we are not confident in who we are because we're trying to put on an act for our followers. So, confidence. That's the word of the day.

Be confident in who you are.

Self-confidence is key, and when social media emerged, the importance of having high self-esteem declined. People found comfort in hiding behind the screen of their phone, tablet, or computer, and they became uncomfortable in front of actual people.

Social media gives us the opportunity to put on a show for anyone interested in watching. We can write a status on how we feel, we can post a million photos with our best friends or our favorite ice cream, and we can record snippets of what we're currently doing. Social media has evolved into an amazing outlet for expression. But it has also turned into a false reality for many people. Because we are not recording every second of our lives, we have the luxury of picking and choosing what we share online, and the internet is not a place for insecurities or low self-esteem. I say that with caution.

If you are insecure about yourself, using Facebook to portray a false image only digs a deeper hole in your soul. **Facebook isn't meant to help you face your problems; you have to deal with them in real life.**

One key to being confident is to accept, and not be afraid of rejection. **The day I began to care less about being rejected was the day I felt empowered to take on the world.** There's no use in fearing whether or not people like or accept you. That takes up too much mental space and it does no good for that peace of mind we've been talking about. It sounds much easier said than done, but I mean it when I say this works for me every single day.

I go after ideas that would be considered "out of my league," and I can do so because I know the worst that can happen is someone saying "no" or "I don't like that." So what?! **If someone doesn't like you or what you have to offer, you can't let that defeat you.** There are billions of people on earth - someone is bound to appreciate you and your wonderful talents. Even more, why would you want to be around people who don't appreciate what you have to offer? Now, let me make this clear: this is not to say you should never change who you are - you should always be trying to better yourself. This is also not me saying to disregard constructive criticism. Again, you should always be trying to better yourself. This is me saying **when you are giving your best and showcasing your true self, someone who rejects you won't matter much in your success anyway.** The only way they will be remotely relevant is when you reflect on all the people who doubted you along your journey to success; then you can sit back and kick your feet up with your new pair of Ray Bans because you have it like that. *insert emoji with the sunglasses*

Actually get out and live.

Occasionally, when I'm out having fun, I like to take photos (if I remember) of the moment and post them online right away. But more often than not, I take photos and post them later on when I'm home and settled. This is because I believe in living in the moment. I had a conversation with one of my good friends, and I asked what his favorite quote was. He simply said, "Be here. Now." I have a few favorites, but this is definitely one to live by! When you're out enjoying life, let the moments happen in their most natural way. Don't interrupt your time taking 20 minutes to find the perfect photo to post, while getting sidetracked and scrolling through other people's news feeds. Doing this takes you out of the natural moment, and it stops you from living in the real world for whatever amount of time it takes to finish your social media break. I'm not saying don't ever log onto social media when you're out enjoying life. I'm simply saying, don't let it control your ability to stop, smell the roses, and have a good time in the process. Thinking back, one of my college friends and I would hang out occasionally. She was such a fun person to be around and we always found ourselves laughing together! The only reason I hated hanging out with her more than I enjoyed it was because there was rarely a second when she wasn't recording us on Snapchat, scrolling through Instagram, texting, or updating her status. Capturing a moment is perfectly fine - I know that as an amateur photographer - but ruining the moment with excessive use of social media is not fun for me. Believe me, **you will see a big difference in how you view the world when you leave your phone and your social media accounts alone for a while. Especially when you were only posting to keep up with someone else's lifestyle anyway. *sips tea*.** Remember, confidence is the word of the day, and every day.

Life has so much to offer, but so many people miss out because they are living in a virtual bubble. The bottom line here is to get out, live, breathe, and enjoy all of life's natural and most precious occurrences. Time is one thing you can't get back, so don't waste it trying to be someone else. Be you. Be original. Let's get a little deeper into this confidence conversation, though.

Chapter Checkpoint

"Facebook isn't meant to help you face your problems; you have to deal with them in real life."-**Staci Inez**

Let's be honest here. Why do I really post the things I do on social media? Is it because I want people to think my life is going much better than it is? Am I dealing with insecurity and I use social media as validation to make myself feel better? Or is it because I truly enjoy sharing bits and pieces of my life?

What are three things I can do to place less emphasis on

my virtual life and live more in real moments?

_____

_____

_____

_____

_____

_____

_____

_____

_____

_____

_____

_____

_____

_____

_____

_____

_____

_____

_____

_____

_____

_____

_____

_____

_____

_____

_____

_____

Self Esteem – Leave your problems at the door

"The way people treat you is not a reflection of you, it's a reflection of them."

There's a solid reason why I wanted to separate this chapter from the confidence section in the Supreme Court of Social Media. This is more so for you to understand the effects of having poor self-esteem. We're going to make sure your self-esteem is up to par as well, but we need to take a look at how your life and relationships can be affected if you don't take care of yourself first.

I learned a valuable lesson during the maturing stages of my life, and when I realized this, it changed the way I viewed myself and people: it's that **people will treat you however they want, and turn around and make you look like the problem.** That's why the opening quote in this chapter couldn't be more real. You need to think about this when people are rude or disrespectful to you. You have to be confident enough in yourself to understand when people do you wrong, talk to you in a belittling way, or do anything to make you feel less than, this is not your problem! It wasn't until I was in college that I fully understood this concept, and I know many people today that still don't quite get it, but that's okay because you can tell them to read this book for better clarity! :) Anyway, I used to believe that people would treat me a certain way because of the person I was. By this, I mean I used to think people would treat me with respect because I respected myself and I showed it to other people. This may seem like an obvious no-no to some, but until I started dealing with people who truly weren't happy with themselves, I didn't fully understand.

I remember when I was 13 years old, I was at a birthday

party. I will never forget this one girl at the birthday party who constantly felt the need to remind me that I was skinny. I've been small my entire life, so by age 13, this wasn't news to me. However, she constantly felt like she needed to remind me in the rudest ways how skinny I was. She was rude to me during the entire sleepover and I really couldn't understand why. I knew I was small, but I didn't know why being so small made her feel like she could look down on me. After talking the situation over with a few trusted people, I came to realize that she wasn't happy with her size, so she felt better putting me down because of mine. Surprisingly enough, after dealing with her for more than 48 hours, this still didn't convince me that people's behavior toward me wasn't a reflection of me. I never chose to be small. There was no special routine I had to remain small, and I surely didn't have anything against anyone who wasn't my size. I figured this was a rare occurrence and I vulnerably moved on with life.

As I got older, I matured, and my perspective on life changed. I realized during my teenage years, there were many times when people treated me a certain way or said negative things about my life in a subliminal way that I did not notice at the time. I'm a person that believes in reflection, and when I reflected on some old friendships and relationships, I realized there were more people against me than were for me.

Speaking of relationships, it's always good to pay attention to the way your friends respond to your relationship with a significant other because that can tell you a lot about who they are. Some of your friends may be truly happy for you when they see how happy you are in a relationship, but some of them may never have anything good to say about you. If you are truly happy in your relationship, your friends should be there to support you, not throw jabs every second they get. It's all about how you communicate. So if you want to tell your friend you think their partner is bad for them, tell them you support them FIRST, then give them your opinion in a respectful, supportive way. I'm speaking from experience. I remember dating one guy and someone who I thought was my friend always had such horrible things to say to me about it. He wasn't perfect by any means, but he wasn't completely awful. It didn't seem to matter, though, because every time we celebrated or did something fun with each other, she always had a problem with it. She could not find it in her to be happy for us no matter the occasion, and I could not figure out why. Just like my situation at the birthday party, I realized my "friend" wasn't happy about my relationship because she was having trouble keeping her own. Don't get me wrong, I'm not a cocky person. I don't go around claiming people are jealous of me, but thinking back, envy from not having a solid relationship was the only explanation for her actions. But let's think about this: **If you aren't happy with yourself, you aren't ready for a relationship anyway, because your happiness will be dependent on someone else.** This is why it's so important to check your friends and make sure they have your best interest at heart; if they don't, you won't be able to find them when you need them.

We all know those people; the ones who love to claim they're your friend, but somehow never find it in them to support anything you do. Yet, you think because you guys are friends, they still have your back. I'm sure you can think of at least one person right now that is exactly like this, and you're not quite sure why they don't really support you or why they aren't always cheering you on in your time of need, but you know that something is a little off. Your gut feeling is always right and here's how I see things now: **If your "friends" don't make it obvious that they have your back, they don't. In your time of need, you don't have time to guess who's there for you. Real friends make it known without having to say a word.** It's toxic to have friends in your life who aren't happy with themselves, because that will eventually spill into your life, and they won't find it in them to be truly happy for you. This is why it's important to have high self-esteem and to know yourself and your worth. If I didn't have high self-esteem, that girl from the birthday party we've been talking about would've easily broken me to pieces. If you aren't confident in who you are and you don't know your value, people will take advantage of you. They will knock you down, leave you there, and only reach out to help you up when they see someone else doing it first. Being confident is not always easy when life throws you so many obstacles and you feel overwhelmed. However, one thing I always say about life is that everything is a choice. **You have to choose to win at life or life will choose to knock you down. With that being said, you have to choose confidence every single day.** If you've been struggling with your self-esteem, remember this quote: "change doesn't happen overnight, but it does happen." You can start with something as simple as looking in the mirror and telling yourself "No matter what happens today, I can do this!" The old saying "fake it 'til you make it" will never get old because it's true. If you tell yourself every day, even multiple times a day, that you can handle whatever comes your way, then eventually you will believe it and I'll be darned if you don't start noticing a difference. The change begins with you saying the mantra to yourself each day, but what really changes is your perspective. The more you believe in yourself, the more you will succeed. Think of the most successful person you know and ask them if they got that way by not believing in themselves. I highly doubt the answer will be yes. After each day, take a minute to find something at which you succeeded. It could be anything from passing a test, not cursing out your coworker, or making it to the gym. This is a simple confidence booster, but it allows you to give yourself credit and ultimately boost the way you feel about yourself.

At the beginning of this chapter, I mentioned the effects of having poor self -esteem. The girl at the birthday party is an example of what many people do every single day. You might even be one of these people and not realize it. Don't worry, though. I'm not here to judge. Many people put others down in multiple ways every day because they are not happy or confident about something in their own personal life. Maybe someone isn't happy in their relationship, so they always give you the side eye and try to find something wrong with your relationship. Maybe one of your coworkers is unhappy because they thought they'd be more successful than they currently are, so the fact that you're succeeding pisses them off. You'll be able to spot these people because every time something good happens to you, they always have some snarky thing to say to you. Then, they'll laugh it off as if it were a joke.

Perhaps you know someone who is rude and has a horrible attitude every single day. It's not like when someone is just having a bad day because their bad day seems to be every day. I always say people like this have a deeper issue they haven't addressed and they are taking it out on people they encounter each day. It's so important to take time and learn yourself to avoid this type of behavior. Doing this can easily make you the person nobody likes, and who really wants to be that person?

I've noticed people like this often don't like to admit that something is wrong, so it's hard for them to change. However, the famous saying "leave your problems at the door" could not be any more true. No one else needs to be disrespected by you because you are having personal issues. Suck it up, treat people with respect, and deal with your personal issues without tearing down other people.

The examples are endless, but the point is, people do these things every single day when they're unhappy or lack self-confidence. Check yourself to make sure you aren't treating people with an attitude because of something going on in your personal life as well. Just because you hate your job doesn't mean you should hate on someone else when they get a promotion at their job, regardless of the work they do.

As the opening quote states, "the way people treat you is not a reflection of you, it's a reflection of them."

Even if you feel like someone deserves to be treated poorly because of something they did to you, it's up to you how you act toward them. You can choose to be the "bigger person" and still treat them with respect because you are above the nonsense. But this all goes back to the way you feel about yourself. **It's quite challenging to uplift someone else when you can't even lift yourself. And it's also very easy to disrespect someone when you don't respect yourself.** The point being, whether you want to admit it or not, the way you treat people is a reflection of the way you treat yourself. You have to keep yourself in check and understand that no one else is responsible for your problems. **Life is all about perspective, so if something bad happens to you, don't take it out on other people. Find the learning lesson in the situation and let it make you a better person.** You can't take your problems out on other people and you certainly shouldn't demean others because you're unhappy with your own life. Focus more on being positive and sharing that positive energy with everyone else. Walking around being hateful to people only makes us hate ourselves in the long-run because there is no internal happiness. When you're genuinely happy inside, it will show, and you won't treat people in a way that makes them feel less than.

So, what can we take away from this lesson:

1. The way people treat you is a reflection of them, and not you. The same applies to the way you treat people, as well.

2. Having friends in your life who aren't happy with themselves can become toxic to your life. They may be secretly hoping you fail instead of cheering you on to succeed. Keep your eyes open.

3. You have to choose to win in life or life will choose to knock you down. Confidence is a choice. Believe in yourself! I believe in you!

Chapter Checkpoint

"The way people treat you is not a reflection of you, it's a reflection of them."

It's been said it takes 30 days of repetition for an act to become a habit. What can I repeat to myself each day to keep pushing forward and remain confident in myself? Think of a mantra…

_____

_____

_____

_____

_____

_____

Relationships – Let love grow

"Love is friendship that has caught fire. It is quiet understanding, mutual confidence, sharing and forgiving. It is loyalty through good and bad times. It settles for less than perfection and makes allowances for human weaknesses." -**Ann Landers**

I always say there are three main things that make any relationship successful, be it friends, family, or significant others: communication, trust, and respect. These are *not the only* factors in a successful relationship, but from my experience, having a solid balance of all three will certainly help lead you to healthy relationships. It's important to understand how having unhealthy relationships can lead to the downfall of your well-being, because it can interfere with your job, social life, mental health, and even your money. We, as humans, place a high value on the relationships in our lives and rightfully so. When everything else in the world seems to be crashing down, at least we can look to the person or people closest to us for comfort, support, and the necessary reminder that everything will be okay. It's also important to remember to build a healthy relationship with yourself because it's hard to support other people when you can't even support yourself; whether that's physically, emotionally, financially, etc. You have to know who you are in order to be at your best for other people.

Communication

There is a way to communicate everything, but effective communication takes discipline; it really comes down to how much your relationship means to you. If you value it, there's no excuse not to work at it.

It's important to understand communication goes far beyond the words you choose to say. It's also in your body language, tone of voice, and your ability to listen. The more you understand the person you're with, the better you can communicate with them. It truly takes time to get to know and understand someone, so when you're first starting out, pay attention to them. Getting to know your partner is often a never-ending process, because people are complex, and you can learn something new about them every single day. Here's a simple example of why understanding your partner plays a part in communicating with them: Let's say the person you're with doesn't handle criticism well, and every time you try to give them constructive feedback they get upset with you. It is your job to find a better way to communicate to them in a manner that doesn't come off as criticism. You have to be more careful about the words you say, and make sure your tone is not threatening. You don't want to start off bashing them with things they've done wrong. Even if you are right, that's not the most effective way to get across to them. Of course, the argument can be made on whether or not people should be able to handle constructive criticism, but that's not the point here. This is to say you have to consider your partner in everything you say or do because if you can't communicate effectively, it will lead to misunderstandings. Misunderstandings are usually caused by poor communication, and that can easily turn a small problem into a larger, unnecessary one.

So while we're on the subject, let's go over some housekeeping when it comes to having disagreements with your partner.

Tone: **There's a fine line between having a discussion and having an argument. The key to separating the two is often**

your tone of voice. Many times we get frustrated when trying to hash out a problem with our partner, but as I will continue to say, effective communication takes discipline! That means no matter how mad you are about your partner calling out something you do, you don't need to start yelling or raising your voice. What does that really solve? They could hear you clearly before you started yelling, so doing that is just going to make things worse. The way you talk to your partner is important at all times, but it's especially important when you're confronting a problem. Throwing out smart remarks, having a snarky attitude, raising your voice, or throwing low blows about a person's life are all good ways to avoid actually solving the problem. Sidenote: if you do find yourself in an argument with your partner, it's vital that you don't throw low blows. **There is never a time for attacking sensitive subjects, but it certainly isn't in the middle of an argument, because once the argument is over, your hurtful words will still exist.**

When your partner does something you don't like, it's important to address the issue when it happens. I've learned when people don't do this, they tend to let the behavior continue and the anger from it builds up inside of them. This is unhealthy for the relationship because eventually, the person holding in their problems will get to a breaking point, and the smallest thing will set them off. Early in the relationship it's important to establish what things bother you and what makes you tick, and it's important to *listen* when your partner is telling you these things; it can seriously help eliminate unnecessary issues in the future.

So, let's talk a little more about the concept of listening. Many people don't realize listening is just as important, if not more important, during communication than speaking.

Businessman, author, and educator Stephen Covey once said: "Most people do not listen with the intent to understand; they listen with the intent to reply." He couldn't have said it better! Really think about how often you are hearing someone talk and you're already forming what you're going to say without even listening to them. When your partner is trying to talk to you and you are tuning them out because you're mad at them, the entire conversation is a waste, and whatever problem you were having will not get fixed. I always say **life is too short to spend your time arguing with your partner. Figure out what the problem is, figure out a solution, and move on.** There is no need to leave issues hanging in the air when you can simply address the problem and get back to having fun and loving each other. So, passive aggressive people, listen up. I'm not saying it's easy, either, because some relationship problems are more complicated than others, but that's no excuse not to figure out a solution.

Let's say I asked Justin to drop off an important document today because I had to go to work too early in the morning. Then, let's say he forgot to do it. I'm going to be pissed because I really needed those papers dropped off this morning and he didn't do what I asked and needed of him. I could easily not talk about it and go drop off the papers late, but I'd probably still be upset because I asked him to do one thing, and now *I* look like I can't get things done on time. If I didn't address this issue the first time, and he got in the habit of forgetting to do things I asked, eventually I would get to a breaking point. I would be fed up and as soon as he did something as small as leaving a spoon in the sink, I could flip out over that and cause a huge argument. Now, I'm not going to do those things, but my point is this is how problems escalate for no reason. I let him go on and on without addressing the fact that he never does anything I ask, and he's become comfortable doing it as if it's okay. This could easily turn into a yelling brawl with us going back and forth spitting out things we hate about each other, when in reality, the situation wasn't that big, we just didn't address it when we should've. This is just one example, but I'm sure you can think of a time where you or your partner snapped over something and you found out later it was because of a small issue built up over time.

No matter what the issue is, putting it off, arguing, or not listening to each other will not help you get through it. You both have to be mature when you have problems or disagreements. Like I said in the beginning, effective communication takes discipline. You have to turn off your inner, petty self and understand for the better of the relationship, you need to be mature in addressing issues. When you're telling your partner what they did to upset you, make sure you give examples of what they did to help illustrate the problem. This is also another reason why addressing the issue when it happens is important, so you can point out specific actions, and there's no room for anyone to forget what happened. Make sure you can back up what you're saying if there's an issue, but you need to be prepared to present a solution at the same time. Calling out a problem without having a fix is a waste. You can't expect someone to know what they're doing is a problem; especially if it's something they've been doing long before they knew you existed. In some situations, it can be quite obvious that a person is causing a problem, but in relationships, it's more effective to make everything clear. **No one needs to play mind games with why you're upset. If you have a problem, say something; otherwise, you're prolonging the issue for no reason.**

Let's move away from problem-solving for a second, though. Let's talk about communicating on a more basic level and how that ties into the next topic: **TRUST.**

When you have things going on in your life - things as simple as doctor's appointments, meetings with co-workers, or going to hang out at your friend's house - I've found it to be much more beneficial to communicate these things to your partner. I try to be as open as possible about everything going on in my day because it helps avoid a trust issue. I make sure I tell Justin if I'm going to stop and run errands before coming home from work, or if I'm just going to hang out at Paula's studio for a while. It doesn't matter what it is, I try to always keep him informed. By me sharing the simple things I have going on, he doesn't have to worry about me hiding anything and he doesn't have to wonder what I'm doing when he's not around. He's never once required me to tell him exactly where I am at all times, but in my experience, it's easier to build a strong level of trust when you talk openly about the things going on in your life. I've heard some people say that I'm doing too much or that I should be able to have my privacy, but I simply don't agree. I still maintain a level of privacy if it's necessary, but at the end of the day, when you're with someone, it isn't just about you anymore. I have nothing to hide, so I have no problem telling him everything. If someone calls you, male or female, and your partner hasn't heard of this person before, I would suggest taking time to explain the relationship between you and the person. Maybe it's your old roommate from college that you haven't talked to in a while, or maybe it's your ex from a few years back. Either way, I think it's important to explain "new people," because it shows you aren't afraid to communicate and you are building trust between the two of you. If you have a hard time trusting people, it's going to be even harder for you in a relationship, and in my opinion, you shouldn't get into a relationship if you "don't trust anyone." You cannot bring old problems into a new relationship; it's that simple. **The person you're with now has nothing to do with the fact that you got cheated on in previous relationships.** This is not their problem, and you don't need to make it their problem. **If you <u>choose</u> to be in a relationship, you have to <u>choose</u> to trust your partner until they give you a reason not to.** This is not to say you shouldn't keep an eye open for any suspicious behavior, either. And it's not to say that this is easy to do. It's definitely a challenge trying to trust someone new after you've been betrayed. This is to say you can't go around accusing your partner of cheating every time they do something you're not used to, simply because you have trust problems. In my experience, this will create a lot of frustration for your partner and it will cause many arguments. The first step in any problem-solving situation is to admit the problem. So, if your partner suggests you may have a trust problem, don't get upset with them. Take a step back and take what they said into consideration. They may actually be telling you something you didn't realize about yourself. Again, this is not for the person who is lying to and cheating on their partner; this is for people who are truly committed to making their relationship work. I've been in relationships where I literally had to explain why it was important to have trust. You would think it's common sense for your partner to know that trust is necessary for a successful relationship, right? Well, they knew trust was important, they just didn't care. If you find yourself having to constantly explain or argue about building stronger trust and the other person seems not to care, that could easily be a sign that they cannot be trusted. In my case, that's exactly what happened. It was when I stopped to realize I shouldn't have to make someone care about building trust, that I started paying more and more attention to their behavior and decided the relationship was unhealthy and it wasn't benefitting my life in any way. There are little things you can do each day that can help build the overall level of trust. You can try things as simple as not turning your phone face down when sitting with your partner after getting a text message. Or, obviously ignoring a phone call without saying who it is or why you ignored it; those are just some simple examples. It can seem like a tedious thing to do, but if you're dealing with someone who has trust problems already, you need to do everything you can to help build back the trust, within reason of course. If you are the person who needs to work on your level of trust, it won't be an easy task, but if you're already invested in the relationship, the least you can do is make a conscious effort each day to strengthen that bond between you and your partner, but communication is really the key in doing that.

Again, some people aren't in favor of this concept, and that's okay. I can only say what's worked for me in my experiences, and it's always been easier building trust when I communicate openly. I also see it as a sign of **RESPECT** when you are open with your partner. You should respect them enough as a person to not treat them like they're crazy for wondering where you've been the last four hours after work. **When you respect your partner, certain things just don't happen; you wouldn't put on a single image in front of other people when your partner isn't around if you had respect for them.** That's just an example, though. I'm not saying you have to bring them up in every conversation, but you shouldn't be actively pursuing someone, trying to get their phone number or meet up with them as if you were single and ready to mingle. You get what I mean?

Keep in mind that respecting each other's opinion is sometimes difficult, but it is necessary. You are not always going to agree on everything, but you have to agree to respect the way a person feels. You don't get to decide whether or not you hurt someone's feelings, so if they say you did, respect their opinion and try to understand. I've also noticed when people have been together for years and years, respect can become a problem. People tend to get comfortable and sometimes feel like they don't have to respect their partner anymore because they probably aren't leaving after umpteen years. It's natural for you to get more comfortable in your relationship, but it's not okay for you to stop putting forth the effort. Still work to have a strong, healthy relationship together, and if you have kids, at least put forth the effort to demonstrate what it means to treat people with respect and to demand respect when in a relationship (when they're ready for that of course).

Since we were kids, we've always heard of this thing called The Golden Rule: Treat people the way you want to be treated. Well, my version is a little different. Instead of "treat people the way you want to be treated," I say, "treat people with respect regardless of how you want to be treated." Remember this quote: "The way people treat you is not a reflection of you, it's a reflection of them."

When working on communication, trust, and respect, try doing things as a couple that can strengthen your bond. Justin and I put up a whiteboard one day and wrote down a list of things we wanted to do as a team; things like cycling, swimming, golfing, exercising, volunteering, etc. We are working on doing everything on the list, but one thing that brought us closer was deciding to volunteer. We served as mentors for teenagers, helping them with school work, starting their own businesses, teaching them life lessons, and just showing them a positive way of life together. This helped change our perspective on life and it made our bond stronger because we were apart of something bigger than ourselves. We absolutely loved working with the teenagers, and no matter what problems we may have had that day, they were put aside because it wasn't about us anymore. Sit down with your partner and talk about what you both enjoy doing, and work on a plan to do some of those things together. Exercising with your partner is also important for Justin and I. It allows us to push each other and hold each other accountable, while also having a good time. When you work out with someone you already enjoy being around, it usually makes the workout more fun. There are plenty of couples exercises online that can get you started, or you can simply start by jogging together twice a week. Whatever you want to do, just try it out and see if it makes a difference. The key to making this successful, though, is making sure to commit. Be serious about doing things together and don't make excuses for why you can't. If something comes up that may get in the way of you and your partner's routine, **communicate** and let them know what's going on. But at least put forth the effort to spend more time together aside from sitting on the couch watching TV.

As I said before, communication, trust, and respect are not the only three things that will create a successful relationship, but I've learned that you have a much better shot if you can find a healthy balance of each one. There's no perfect formula for relationships; you really have to figure out what works best for you and your partner.

Take this with you as we finish up our talk about relationships: "Being alone may scare you, but being in a bad relationship will damage you." –Anonymous

Chapter Checkpoint

*"Love is friendship that has caught fire. It is quiet understanding, mutual confidence, sharing and forgiving. It is loyalty through good and bad times. It settles for less than perfection and makes allowances for human weaknesses." -***Ann Landers**

Who are the most important people in my life?

_____
_____
_____
_____
_____
_____
_____
_____
_____
_____
_____

What steps can I take *each day* to strengthen the relationships between me and all of these people? Can I call someone more? Could I stop by and see how someone is doing? Write down some key steps and actually follow through with them.

_____
_____
_____

The end is only the beginning

"Look deep into nature. Then you will understand everything better." -**Albert Einstein**

As I wind down the tales of this book, I'd like to, first, thank you for sticking with me through the entire story. I certainly appreciate it. I hope you found at least one thing in this book that was valuable to your life. I am still a work-in-progress, but I certainly believe as long as you continue working on yourself, you will see positive results. Life is too short to spend it unhappy and bitter inside. As I've said before, it's not always easy to know when your actions are reflecting internal unhappiness, but that's why it's so important to get to know yourself. You have to get to know yourself just like you would any other person you're trying to a build a relationship with. I encourage you to spread positivity everywhere you go. No matter how hard your day is, don't take it out on someone else. Keep your head up and know things are going to get better. Remember this: **There may be stressors in your life, but you don't have to let them stress you out. Being stressed is a choice, and it's all in how you view your situation.** Here's one final example of how I manage to remain calm and keep my peace of mind, even when I get really mad about something.

I always say nature reveals the beauty of being at peace. It took me a long time to understand this concept, but when I realized just how peaceful nature really is, I began to appreciate the simple things in life. I absolutely love being outdoors, and that is also why I hate cold weather, because I want to be comfortable outside all the time. I love taking a walk on a trail, hiking, kayaking, walking through gardens, sitting by the lake or enjoying the ocean. But it wasn't until I began to appreciate the natural beauty of the world that I realized the value of being connected to nature. When I was younger, I started going to the lake when I got really upset about something. I would sit by the water and write until no more thoughts could come from my mind onto paper. I would write about whatever bothered me in the first place, but I would usually go on to talk about my future, what I want out of life, or practically anything that came to mind. I would just let my mind and hands work without putting much thought into it. I've said many times before that my main goal in life is to have inner peace and happiness. I say this because nothing else I want to accomplish in life can be done without being at peace with myself and without being happy with the life I have. Sitting by the lake was very calming, and it allowed me to understand the value of simplicity. That is why I say nature reveals the beauty of being at peace. Even though I originally started writing at the lake whenever I was mad about something, it really became a part of my routine and I started writing by the lake whenever I wanted, not just when things weren't going well. This is where my goal for inner peace and happiness was developed because I realized no matter what happened in life, I can't escape myself, so I need to do everything I can to make sure I love the person I am. Only then will I be able to reach my full potential in achieving the goals I set for myself. I encourage you to take some time and write down everything you've ever wanted to accomplish, no matter how far-fetched it may seem. Write it all down, and write down what it's going to take for you to make those goals come to life. **Understand that everything worth having is worth waiting for, but if you don't put in the work, you'll be waiting forever.** Never stop believing in yourself and always look for ways to become a better person. I hope you find everything you're searching for in this life, and I wish you nothing but the best. Thank you, again, for sharing your valuable time with me. I truly appreciate it.

Peace and love.

-Staci

Final Checkpoint

How can I proactively become more at peace with myself and gain a sense of overall happiness? Write freely to express any final thoughts after reading this book.

Remember, happiness starts within; create it.

_____

_____

_____

_____

_____

_____

_____

_____

_____

_____

_____

_____

_____

_____

_____

_____

_____

_____

_____

_____

www.ingramcontent.com/pod-product-compliance
Lightning Source LLC
LaVergne TN
LVHW051200080426
835508LV00021B/2722